THE Music CONNECTION

PROGRAM AUTHORS

Jane Beethoven
Dulce Bohn
Patricia Shehan Campbell
Carmen E. Culp
Jennifer Davidson
Lawrence Eisman
Sandra Longoria Glover
Charlotte Hayes

Martha Hilley
Mary E. Hoffman
Sanna Longden
Hunter March
Bill McCloud
Marvelene Moore
Catherine Nadon-Gabrion
Mary Palmer

Carmino Ravosa
Mary Louise Reilly
Will Schmid
Carol Scott-Kassner
Jean Sinor
Sandra Stauffer
Judith Thomas

RECORDING PRODUCERS

Darrell Bledsoe
Jeanine Levenson

J. Douglas Pummill
Buryl Red, Executive Producer

Linda Twine
Ted Wilson

SILVER BURDETT GINN

PARSIPPANY, NJ   NEEDHAM, MA

Atlanta, GA   Deerfield, IL   Irving, TX   San Jose, CA

ISBN 0-382-26180-1

5 6 7 8 9 -VH- 99 98 97

C · O · N · T

CONCEPTS

THEMES

·E·N·T·S

READING

REFERENCE BANK

"The" Beat

In My Feet

The Playtime Beat

It rained a mist

Man with a Green Beard   by Karl Schmidt–Rottluff

Aaron by Thomas Hart Benton

Peas

Sweet
Potatoes

Tomatoes

Cabbage

I Sing Through the Day

Cock - a - doo - dle, doo - dle, doo.

Whispers of Wishes

Sounds of All My Friends

'Round and 'round, we must go,

Sally Walker (Detail)   by Brenda Joysmith

Medicine Dancers by Cecil Youngfox

I got a house in Bal - ti - more,

Brus-sels car-pet on the floor,

I got a house in Bal - ti - more,

Street-car runs right by my door,

SERVICE 102

Deer and Maple Tree, c. 1810   Mori Shushin Tessan

A Piece of Silly Pie

1. eyes
2. nose
3. ears
4. voice
5. fingers
6. toes

44

I like to **eat**

I like to **ate**

I like to **ete**

I like to **ite**

I like to **ote**

I like to **ute**

I like to eat.

Going to a Concert

Songs
to End Our Day

Ay-lye, lyu-lye

Yiddish Folk Song   *English Words by Richard Morris*

Ay - lye, lyu - lye, lyu - lye,

Go to sleep now, don't cry;

Close your eyes in slum - ber,

Oh, my dar - ling kind' - lach.

A Book Is a Magic Carpet

African Noel

Liberian Folk Song   Collected and Translated by Aden G. Lewis

Sing   No - el,   sing   No - el,

Fine

No - el,   No - el. _____

Sing   No - el,   sing   No - el,

D.C. al Fine

No - el,   No - el. _____

The Nutcracker

Mail Myself to You

I'm gonna wrap myself
in

I'm gonna daub myself
with

Stick some
on top of my head,

I'm gonna mail myself
to you.

I'm a–gonna tie me up in a

I'm gonna tie too;

I'm a–gonna climb up in my

I'm gonna mail myself to you.

Words and music by Woody Guthrie

Footprints and Shadows

Touch the Beat

Engine, Engine

How Many Sounds on a Beat?

SO and MI

so

mi

so

mi

SO

mi

so   so

mi

Can You Find It?

Songs with *SO* and *MI*

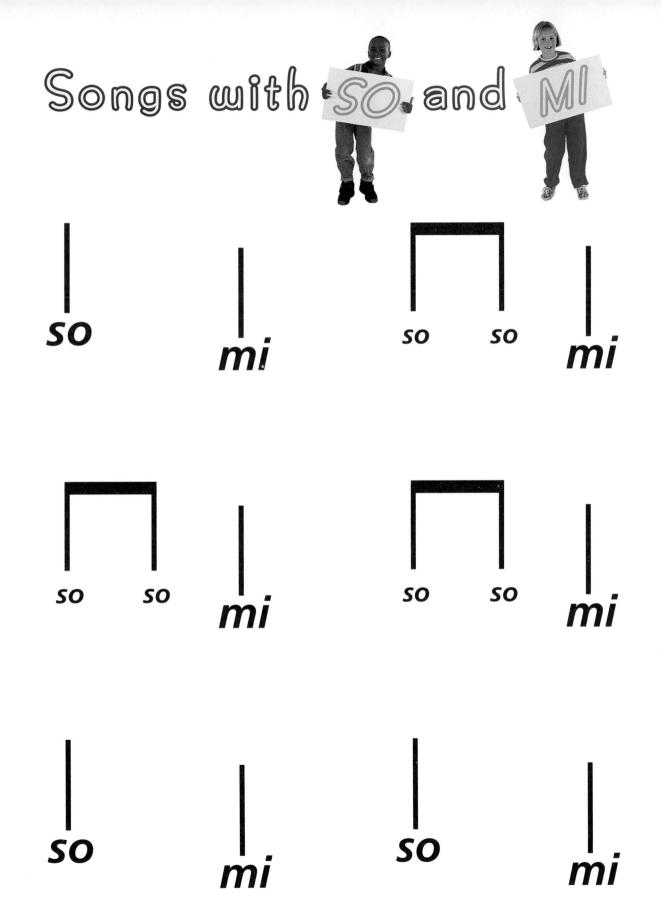

so   mi   so   so   mi

so   so   mi   so   so   mi

so   mi   so   mi

Lines and Spaces

Line 5

Line 4

Line 3

Line 2

— Line 1

Space 4

Space 3

Space 2

Space 1

Writing Stems

Stems That Go Down

Singing and Playing Melodies

Using *SO*, *MI*, and ?

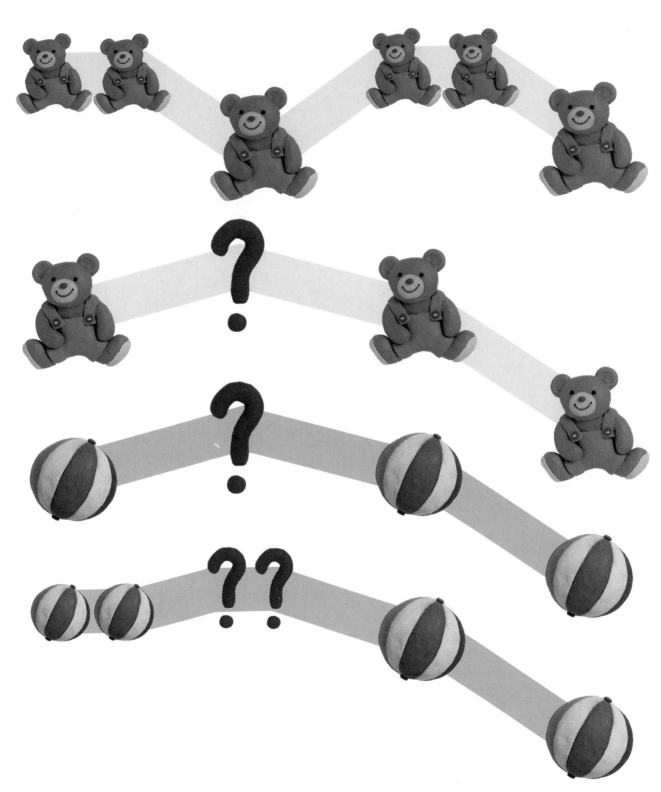

Finding a
New Note

LA

| so | mi | so | mi |

| so | so | ? | ? | so | so | mi |

| so | so | mi | so | so | mi |

| so | ? | so | mi |

Stems For *SO, MI,* and *LA*

Accents in Two

so   la   so   mi

so so la la so mi

so   mi la so mi

so so mi la so mi

Conducting in Two

A Rhythm Game

84

The *SO, MI, DO* Family

Ledger Lines

Little Black Bug

Music by Ruth Boshkoff   Words by Margaret Wise Brown

Where   have you been? "I've been

un - der the   rug,"   said the

lit - tle black   bug.

"Bug,   Ugh!   Ugh!"

On a Log, Mister Frog

Traditional

On a log, Mis - ter Frog,

sang his song the whole day long,

Glumf, glumf, glumf, glumf.

Collected and adapted by Katalin Forrai and Jean Sinor

Sound Bank

Song Index

Photograph and Illustration Credits

Acknowledgements

Every effort has been made to locate all copyright holders of materials used in this book. If any errors or omissions have occurred, corrections will be made.

Photograph and Illustration Credits

All photographs are by Silver Burdett Ginn (SBG) unless otherwise noted.

Cover: Dralene "Red" Hughes

2-3: Mary Thelen. 3: *r.* Elliott Varner Smith for SBG. 4: SBG, courtesy of Oshkosh B'Gosh ; *ill.* Seth Larson. 5: *t.l.* Michael Medici/Sonlight Images for SBG; *t.r.* Courtesy, Delta Music *b.l.* Kugler/FPG International; *b.r.* Bob Daemmrich/Tony Stone Images. 6-7: Jody Jobe. 10-11: Cindy Salans Rosenheim. 12-13: Randy Verougstrate. 14-15: Eldon Doty. 16: *t.l.* Peter Lamberti/Tony Stone Images; *t.r.* Breck P. Kent/Animals, Animals; *b.l., b.r.* SuperStock; *ill.* Liisa Chauncy Guida. 17: Leo Monahan. 18-19: Benjamin Vicent. 20: FourByFive/SuperStock; *ill.* Rollin Richter. 21: Steve Bjorkman. 23: Tom Tonkin. 26: *t.l.* J. Traver/Gamma/Liaison; *t.r.* ©1989 Jack Vartoogian; *m.* Brown Brothers; *b.l.* Steve Vidler/Leo De Wys, Inc.; *b.r.* Mercury Archives/The Image Bank. 27: Liisa Chauncy Guida. 28: Jeff Nishinaka. 29: *boy* David Young-Wolff/Tony Stone Images; *girl* Rex Butcher/TonyStone Images. 30: courtesy of Oakview School, Nutley, NJ; *t.r.* David Young-Wolff/Tony Stone Images; *b.l.* Miguel A. Gandert for SBG. 32-33: Sandra Speidel. 35: *background*: Craig Tuttle/The Stock Market; *insets: t.* Elliott Varner Smith for SBG; *b.* Paul Barton/The Stock Market. 39: streetcar courtesy of LTC (ret.) Wm. G. Byrne, Jr. 40-41: Robin Hotchkiss. 42: Ron Thomas/FPG International; *ill.* Gwen Connelly. 44: Jackie Snider. 45: Olivia. 46-47: Gwen Connelly. 48-49: Winifred Barnum Newman. 50-51: Michael Radencich. 54: Steve Hickey. 54-55: *ill.* Lorraine Shirkus. 55: courtesy, The Morris Museum and FRIENDLY'S Ice Cream Shop, Convent Station, N.J. 56: *t.* Phil Borges/Tony Stone Images; *b.l.* Eve Arnold/Magnum; *b.r.* FPG International. 57: *t.l.* Ann Nielsen/Gamma Liaison; *t.r.* Elliott Varner Smith for SBG; *b.* Lori Adamski Peek/ Tony Stone Images. 59: Pamela Becker. 61: *t.l.* Obremski/The Image Bank; *t.r.* Lawrence Migdale; *b.* Elliott Varner Smith for SBG. 62: The Joffrey Ballet's production of THE NUTCRACKER, photo ©Herbert Migdoll; *ill.* Barbara Lambase. 64-65: Kat Thacker. 66-67: FOOTPRINTS AND SHADOWS by Anne Westcott Dodd. Illustrations by Henri Sorenson. ©1992. Used by permission of Simon & Schuster Books for Young Readers; *border ill.* Liz Conrad. 68: Elliott Varner Smith for SBG; *ill.* Doreen Gay Kassel. 69: Doreen Gay Kassel. 70-71: Doreen Gay Kassel. 74: Terry Powell. 75: Doreen Gay Kassel. 76: Doreen Gay Kassel. 77: Jack Graham. 79: Doreen Gay Kassel. 84: Geraldo Suzan. 87: Darius Detwiler. 88-89: Jack Graham.

Sound Bank Photos: 91: *Cabaca-* The Shrine to Music Museum/University of South Dakota; *Native American ankle bells-* The Mathers Museum.

"SALLY WALKER", Pastel by Brenda Joysmith, copyright 1987. All Rights Reserved.